LOUISA M. ALCOTT

Little Women

Retold by Anne Collins

GW00587580

HEINEMANN ELT

BEGINNER LEVEL

Series Editor: John Milne

The Heinemann ELT Guided Readers provide a choice of enjoyable reading material for learners of English. The series is published at five levels – Starter, Beginner, Elementary, Intermediate and Upper. At **Beginner Level,** the control of content and language has the following main features:

Information Control
The stories are written in a fluent and pleasing style with straightforward plots and a restricted number of main characters. The cultural background is made explicit through both words and illustrations. Information which is vital to the story is clearly presented and repeated where necessary.

Structure Control
Special care is taken with sentence length. Most sentences contain only one clause, though compound sentences are used occasionally with the clauses joined by the conjunctions 'and', 'but', and 'or'. The use of these compound sentences gives the text balance and rhythm. The use of Past Simple and Past Continuous Tenses is permitted since these are the basic tenses used in narration and students must become familiar with these as they continue to extend and develop their reading ability.

Vocabulary Control
At **Beginner Level** there is a controlled vocabulary of approximately 600 basic words, so that students with a basic knowledge of English will be able to read with understanding and enjoyment. Help is also given in the form of vivid illustrations which are closely related to the text.

For further information on the full selection of Readers at all five levels in the series, please refer to the Heinemann Readers catalogue.

Contents

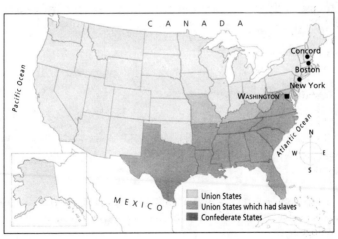

Map of America 1861

A Note About the Author

Louisa May Alcott was American. She was born on 29th November 1832. She lived in the town of Concord, Massachusetts in the east of North America. Louisa's father was Amos Bronson Alcott. He was a teacher and a philosopher. Louisa had three sisters – May, Elizabeth and Anna.

Louisa did not go to school. She learnt her lessons in her home. She was intelligent. She liked books. Louisa read all the books in her father's library. She also talked with her father's friends, Ralph Waldo Emerson, Henry Thoreau and Nathaniel Hawthorne. These men were writers and poets.

Louisa wrote her first story in 1863. She wrote poems and stories for books and magazines. Louisa's most popular book was *Little Women* (1868). The book is about four girls – Amy, Meg, Beth and Jo. Louisa Alcott was writing about her own life and about her sisters. Amy is May Alcott. Meg is Elizabeth Alcott. Beth is Anna Alcott. Jo is Louisa herself.

Louisa wrote a second part to the story, *Little Women*. In America, the book was called 'Part Second'. In England, the book was called *Good Wives* (1869). Other stories by this author are: *An Old-*

4

Fashioned Girl (1870), *Little Men* (1871), *Eight Cousins* (1875), *Rose in Bloom* (1876), *Jo's Boys* (1886).

Louisa Alcott never married. She visited Europe in 1871. When she returned to America she lived in Boston. She worked for women's rights. She often wrote about the lives of independent women. Louisa May Alcott died in Boston on 6th March 1888.

A Note About This Story

Time: 1862 to 1863. **Place**: Massachusetts, in the north-east of the United States. There is a civil war in the USA. Americans are fighting against Americans.

———

In 1860, Abraham Lincoln became President of the United States. Lincoln came from the State of Illinois, in the north of the country. For many years men, women and children had been taken from their homes in Africa. They were taken to America by ship. They were bought by farmers in the southern states of the USA. And they became slaves. They worked on the farms. Cotton, tobacco and sugar were grown on the farms. Slaves were not paid.

The Government of the United States – the Union – wanted to stop slavery. But most people in the south wanted to keep their slaves. In 1861, eleven states in the south joined together. They were called the Confederate States. The Confederate States left the Union. They fought a war. This was called the

American Civil War. The war started in April 1861 and it lasted for four years. The Union in the north had more men, more power and more weapons. But the people of the south were brave and their leaders were strong. The Union Army had 2 200 000 soldiers. 600 000 soldiers died. The Confederate Army had 800 000 soldiers. And 400 000 soldiers died. Many men were put into prison camps. Prison camps were terrible places. There was not much food or medicine. Thousands of men became ill and died. The Confederate Army lost the war. The Union Army won the Civil War in 1865. All the slaves were free.

There were no electric lights at this time. People had oil lamps to light their homes. There were no cars. People rode horses. Or they travelled in carriages pulled by horses. But there were railways in eastern America. In the American Civil War many soldiers travelled on the railway trains. They could reach battles quickly. Reporters wrote about the battles for their newspapers. Then they sent their reports to the newspapers very quickly. They did this by telegrams. Telegraph companies sent these messages through an electric wire. Letters took many days to arrive. But telegrams arrived in a few hours.

The family in this story lives in a small house. They are poor. Mrs March is taking care of her four daughters. Mr March is with the Union Army in Washington. He is not a soldier. He is too old to fight. But he is working in a hospital.

The People in This Story

Mrs March ('Marmee')
ˈmɪsɪz mɑːtʃ (ˈmɑːmiː)

Meg March
meg mɑːtʃ

Jo March
dʒəʊ mɑːtʃ

Beth March
beθ mɑːtʃ

Amy March
ˈeɪmi mɑːtʃ

Mr Laurence
mɪstə ˈlɒrəns

Laurie Laurence
ˈlɒri ˈlɒrəns

John Brooke
dʒɒn brʊk

Dr Bangs
ˈdɒktə bæŋz

Aunt March
ɑːnt mɑːtʃ

Mr March
ˈmɪstə mɑːtʃ

1
The March Sisters

The place was a small town in Massachusetts, North America. It was a cold evening in December 1862. Snow was falling softly.

In the living-room of a small house, four sisters were sitting by the fire. Their names were Meg, Jo, Beth and Amy March. Meg was sixteen years old. Jo was fifteen. Beth was thirteen years old and Amy was twelve.

Their mother, Mrs March, was not in the house. She was visiting a poor, sick family. Their father, Mr March, was far away from home. It was wartime. Mr March was working in a hospital for soldiers.

The four sisters were knitting with wool. They were knitting socks for the soldiers. They worked and they talked.

'We are poor,' said Meg, the eldest girl. 'It is terrible.' Meg was very pretty. She had large eyes and soft brown hair.

'Other girls have lots of pretty things,' said Amy, the youngest girl. Amy had golden hair and blue eyes.

'I hate girls' work and girls' things,' said Jo. She was tall and thin. She had beautiful, long red hair. 'I don't want to stay at home,' she said. 'I want to fight in the war.'

Then Beth spoke. 'Yes, we are poor,' she said. 'But we are lucky too. We have Father and Mother and we have each other.'

Beth was very shy. She was afraid of strangers but she loved her family very much.

'Yes, we have each other,' said Jo. And the girls were happy again.

'It's six o'clock!' said Meg. 'Be quick, everybody! Mother is coming! We must get supper ready.'

Jo brought more wood for the fire. Meg lit the lamps. Beth and Amy put the food on the table.

The door opened and Mrs March came into the room. Mrs March was not beautiful but she was very kind and good. Her daughters had a special name for her. They called her 'Marmee'.

'How are you, my dears?' said Mrs March. 'Did you have a good day?'

'Yes, thank you, Marmee,' replied the four sisters.

'Come. Sit down by the fire, Marmee,' said Meg. 'Supper is ready.'

After supper, Mrs March said, 'Girls, I have a wonderful surprise.'

Everybody was excited.

'Is it a letter from Father?' asked Jo.

'Yes,' replied Mrs March. 'Father has a Christmas message for all of you.'

The girls read their father's letter.

To my four little women

My dears,

I will not see you again for a long time. I think of you all every day. Take care of your mother. Be good and work hard.

Happy Christmas from your loving Father.

2

A Wonderful Christmas

A few days later it was Christmas Day. On Christmas morning, the girls woke early. Each girl had one present – a book from their mother. They ran downstairs. They wanted to thank her. But Mrs March was not there.

A special Christmas breakfast was on the table. There was lots of food and everybody was hungry. But the girls waited for their mother. They waited nearly an hour. At last, their mother came home.

'Merry Christmas, Marmee!' the girls shouted. 'Come. Sit down. Let's eat breakfast.'

'Merry Christmas, little daughters!' said Mrs March. 'Listen! I have something to tell you. There is a poor woman – Mrs Hummel. She lives in the town. She has seven children – one is a baby. The Hummels' house is very cold and they have no food. Will you give them a Christmas present? Will you give them your breakfast?'

All the girls were very hungry. For a moment, nobody spoke.

Then Jo said, 'Yes, we will, Marmee. Let's take the food to them now.'

It was early morning and it was cold. The girls walked quickly through the snow. They carried baskets of food and wood for the fire.

The Hummel family lived in one small room. The

room was in a house near a river. The windows of the room were broken and there was no fire. Mrs Hummel lay in her bed. She was ill. The baby was crying and the children were cold and hungry.

The Hummel children saw the March sisters and the baskets of food. They shouted happily.

'Thank you, thank you!' they shouted.

The girls made a fire and they put the food on the table. Mrs March made some tea. Soon the room was warm. The hungry children ate the food and they laughed.

Later, Mrs March and her daughters went home. They had bread and milk for breakfast. But they were very happy.

The March sisters often acted in plays. Jo wrote the plays. The girls acted in a small room at the top of the house. They put on brightly-coloured clothes and they enjoyed themselves.

On Christmas evening, the girls acted in a play. All their friends came. Everybody enjoyed the play.

Later, their friends went home and the girls had a lovely surprise. Mrs March called to them.

'Supper is ready,' she said.

The girls ran downstairs. They saw lots of delicious food on the table – cakes, sweets, fruit and ice-cream.

'Where did this lovely food come from, Marmee?' Amy asked.

Mrs March smiled. 'Old Mr Laurence sent it,' she replied.

'Old Mr Laurence, our neighbour?' asked Meg. She was surprised. 'But we don't know him,' she said.

'He heard about your breakfast,' said Mrs March. 'He has sent you a special Christmas supper.'

The girls looked at each other.

'This is a wonderful Christmas,' Beth said.

3

Laurie

Next to the Marches' small house, there was a large house. The sisters called this house, 'The Laurence House'. It belonged to their neighbour, Mr Laurence.

Mr Laurence was old and he was very rich. His house was very beautiful. He lived in the house with his grandson. His grandson was fifteen – the same age as Jo. Sometimes the March sisters saw Mr Laurence's grandson. But the boy was always alone.

A few days after Christmas, Jo was in her garden. She was wearing boots and an old coat. Jo was busy. She was sweeping snow from the path with a broom. Jo looked up at the Laurence House. She saw a face looking out of a window. It was Mr Laurence's grandson.

'The boy is sad. He is lonely,' thought Jo.

Then she had an idea. She took some snow and she made a ball with it. She threw the ball at the window. The boy laughed and he opened the window.

'Hello!' called Jo. 'Are you ill?'

'I was ill last week,' said the boy. 'I'm better now, but I'm very bored. I am not doing anything.'

'I'll visit you!' said Jo.

'Yes, please come,' said the boy.

A few minutes later, Jo knocked on the door of the Laurence House. She was carrying a small basket. The basket was full of apples and cakes.

The boy opened the door and Jo gave him the basket.

'These things are for you,' she said. 'They are from my mother.'

'Thank you very much,' said the boy. 'Please come in. My name is Laurie. And you're Jo, aren't you?'

'Yes,' said Jo. She was very surprised. 'How do you know my name?'

'I know your name,' said Laurie. 'I know all your sisters' names. You call to each other in your garden.'

'Sometimes, I see you with your mother,' Laurie said sadly. 'I have no mother. My parents are dead. So I live here with my grandfather. But my grandfather is not at home today.'

'Laurie is rich but he's very lonely,' thought Jo. 'I am poor. But I have a family and I have a happy home.'

'Please visit us,' said Jo 'We are neighbours. Let's be friends too.'

Jo and Laurie talked all afternoon. Jo talked about her family. Laurie talked about his life. He did not go to school. A teacher, Mr Brooke, came to the house every day. Mr Brooke taught Laurie his lessons.

'Come into our library,' said Laurie. 'We have many fine books in the library.'

The library was a beautiful room with big windows. There were hundreds of interesting books on the shelves. There were many fine pictures on the walls.

'What a wonderful room!' said Jo.

Suddenly, Laurie and Jo heard a noise.

'Grandfather has come home,' said Laurie. 'I must go to him. Please stay here.'

Laurie went out of the library. Jo stood by the fire. There was a picture of old Mr Laurence on the wall. Jo looked at the picture. The door of the library opened but she did not turn round.

'Laurie,' she said. 'Mr Laurence – your grandfather is not handsome. But he has a kind face. I like him.'

'Thank you,' said a voice.

Jo turned round quickly. Mr Laurence was standing near the door.

'Oh—' she said. 'I am sorry.'

'So, I'm not handsome?' asked Mr Laurence.

'Well – no, sir.'

'But I have a kind face?'

'Yes, you do, sir,' replied Jo.

Mr Laurence laughed. 'I knew your grandfather,' he said. 'He was a good man. Now, have some tea.'

Laurie was very happy. Laurie and Jo drank tea and they talked. Mr Laurence watched them.

'My grandson is happy,' he thought. 'He was lonely. He must have some friends.'

Later, Jo went home. She told her mother and her sisters about the Laurences' beautiful house.

'Marmee, please let Laurie visit us,' she said.

'Yes, dear,' replied Mrs March. 'Your new friend Laurie will be welcome in our house.'

4

A Present for Beth

Laurie and the March sisters became good friends. They visited each other often. They had many happy days together.

Everybody liked Laurie and his grandfather. Meg, Jo and Amy all went to the Laurence House. Meg loved flowers and gardens. She liked the garden at the Laurence House very much. It was winter and there were no flowers. But there was snow on the trees. They were very beautiful.

Jo wrote plays and stories. And she loved books. She liked the library at the Laurence House. Amy liked the library too. She painted pictures. She liked the paintings on the library walls.

But Beth did not visit the Laurence House. She was very shy. She was afraid of old Mr Laurence.

Beth did not go to school. She learnt her lessons at home. Beth's life was quiet, but she was very happy. She helped her mother with the housework. She learnt her lessons every day.

Beth loved music. The Marches had a piano, but it was very old. Beth tried to play the piano. But the music did not sound very good.

One day, Mr Laurence spoke to Mrs March.

'Do your daughters play the piano?' he asked.

'Beth plays the piano,' Mrs March replied.

'I have a beautiful piano,' said Mr Laurence. 'But nobody plays it now. Will Beth come to my house? Will she play the piano?'

'Beth is very shy,' Mrs March said.

'Laurie and I are often out of the house,' said Mr Laurence. 'Beth must come then. We will not hear her playing the piano.'

Mrs March told Beth the news. Beth was very happy and excited. She wanted to play Mr Laurence's piano.

The next day, Beth went to the Laurence House. The house was very quiet.

'Good,' thought Beth. 'Everybody is out of the house.'

The piano was in the living-room. Beth walked very quietly into the room. She touched the piano.

'How beautiful it is,' she thought.

Some pages of music were lying on top of the piano. Beth looked at the pages. The music was not difficult. So she started to play.

Beth played the piano for many hours. She enjoyed herself very much.

After that, she went to the Laurence House every day. Sometimes, Mr Laurence was in the house. He often listened to the music. But Beth never saw him.

———

A few weeks passed. One day, Beth spoke to her mother.

'Marmee,' she said. 'I want to thank Mr Laurence. He has been very kind. I will give him a present. Shall I knit a pair of slippers for him?'

'Yes, Beth,' replied Mrs March. 'That's a very good idea.'

Beth bought some wool and she made a beautiful pair of slippers. She took them to the Laurence House. Mr Laurence was away from home. So Beth wrote a short note. She put the note and the slippers on a table. Then she went home.

There was no reply from Mr Laurence that day.

22

'Oh,' thought Beth. 'Mr Laurence did not like the slippers.'

The next morning, Beth walked by the river. She was sad. Later, she went home. Her sisters were waiting. They were very excited.

'Beth! Beth! Come quickly,' they called. 'You have a present. Come and see!'

They took Beth into the living-room. In the middle of the room was a beautiful little piano. On top of the piano, there was an envelope.

'Open the envelope, Beth!' said Jo.

'Please open it for me,' said Beth.

Jo opened the envelope. She pulled out a note. She read it to her mother and sisters.

Dear Miss March,

I have had many pairs of slippers. But your slippers are the best. Thank you for your wonderful present.

Here is a present from me. Please enjoy it.

Your good friend, James Laurence

Beth was very excited.

'Mr Laurence has given me this piano,' she said. 'I am very lucky.'

Beth sat down at the piano and started to play. The piano sounded beautiful. But suddenly, she stopped playing.

'I must thank Mr Laurence now,' she said.

Beth was not shy any more. She ran quickly to the Laurence House and went inside. Mr Laurence was in the library. Beth ran to him and she kissed him.

Then she said, 'Dear Mr Laurence! Thank you so much for my beautiful piano.'

Beth was not afraid of Mr Laurence any more.

5

Amy in Trouble

It was Saturday afternoon. Meg and Jo were in their bedroom. They were putting on their coats. They were going out.

Amy came into the bedroom.

'Where are you going?' she asked.

'Don't ask questions!' said Jo.

'We're going to the theatre with Laurie,' said Meg. 'We're going to see a play.'

'Oh!' said Amy. 'I want to come with you. Please!'

'No,' said Jo. 'You are too young.'

'I'm not too young,' she said. 'I'm twelve years old. Please, please let me come with you.'

Jo often became angry very quickly. She became very angry with Amy.

'No, Amy,' she said. 'We will not take you with us. Please go away!'

Amy started to cry. At that moment, Laurie arrived at the house.

'Meg! Jo! Are you ready?' he shouted.

'We're coming!' Jo replied.

Jo and Meg ran downstairs. Amy stopped crying.

'You'll be sorry, Jo March!' she shouted.

Jo and Meg had a wonderful time at the theatre. They returned home in the evening. Amy was reading a book. She did not ask them questions about the play.

———

The next day, Meg, Beth and Amy were sitting in the living-room. They were sitting by the fire. Suddenly, Jo ran into the room. She was very upset.

'Where is my book of stories?' she asked her sisters. 'Have you seen it?'

Jo often wrote stories. She wrote them all in a little book. But today, she could not find her book.

'I haven't seen your book,' said Meg. 'Have you seen it, Beth?'

'No,' said Beth.

Amy was very quiet. She did not say anything.

'Amy, where is my book of stories?' asked Jo.

'I don't know,' replied Amy.

'Yes, you do know!' said Jo. 'Tell me immediately! Where is it?'

'You'll never see it again,' said Amy.

'Why not?' asked Jo.

'I burnt it,' said Amy. 'You didn't let me come to the theatre yesterday. So I threw your book of stories on the fire.'

Jo was very angry. She held Amy's arms and shouted at her.

'You bad, bad girl!' Jo shouted. 'I wrote those stories for Father. Now they are gone for ever.'

Suddenly, Amy was sorry. She started to cry.

'Please forgive me, Jo,' Amy said. 'I'm very, very sorry.' Tears fell from her eyes.

'I'll never forgive you,' said Jo. 'Never!'

Jo did not speak to Amy again that day. She was very angry and upset.

———

The next day, the weather was very cold. There was a river near the Marches' house. The river had frozen. It was ice.

Laurie came to the Marches' house. He was carrying a pair of ice-skates.

'Let's go to the river, Jo!' he said. 'We'll skate on the ice.'

'All right,' replied Jo. She went to a cupboard and she took out her ice-skates.

Amy watched her sister. After a few minutes, Jo and Laurie left the house.

'I want to skate too,' Amy said to Meg.

'Take your ice-skates and run after Jo,' said Meg. 'Jo will enjoy herself. She will soon be happy. Ask her to be your friend again.'

'That is a good idea,' said Amy. She ran after Jo and Laurie. The river was not far away. Soon she saw Jo and Laurie skating on the ice.

The ice was very thin in the middle of the river.

Don't go to the middle of the river, Jo!

Jo heard Laurie's words. But Amy did not hear Laurie. She skated to the middle of the river.

Suddenly, there was a loud CRACK!
The ice broke. Amy was in the water.

Jo was terribly afraid. But she followed Laurie. They pulled Amy from the river. Amy was not hurt but she was very cold and frightened.

Jo and Laurie took Amy home. Mrs March carried Amy upstairs to her bedroom. She took off the little girl's wet clothes. And she wrapped her in a blanket. Then she carried her downstairs to the living-room. Amy fell asleep by the warm fire.

'Will Amy be all right, Marmee?' asked Jo.

'Yes, dear,' replied her mother. 'Amy was in trouble. But she will be all right now. She isn't hurt.'

Jo started to cry.

'I was angry with Amy,' said Jo. 'She burnt my book of stories. But now I am very sorry. Sometimes, I become angry too quickly. What shall I do, Marmee? Please help me.'

'Don't cry, Jo,' said Mrs March. 'Remember this day. You won't become angry again.'

'I will remember,' said Jo.

At that moment, Amy opened her eyes and she smiled. She held out her arms towards Jo. The two sisters did not speak. But they kissed and they put their arms round each other. They were friends again.

———

Winter soon passed. Spring came, and then summer. Mrs March and her daughters were happy. But they all wanted to see Mr March again soon.

6

Meg Loses a Glove

Meg, the eldest March sister, was a very pretty girl. Her friends often invited her to parties. Meg enjoyed the parties, but sometimes she was sad. She was sad because her family was poor. Meg's friends lived in fine houses. They had beautiful clothes. But Meg did not have beautiful clothes and lovely things.

One day in July, Meg was at a friend's house. She heard a conversation. Two women were talking – her friend's mother and another woman. They were talking about Meg.

'Meg March is a kind and lovely girl,' said one woman. 'But her family is poor.'

'The Marches live near the Laurences,' said the other woman. 'The Laurences are very rich. Does Mrs March have marriage-plans for her daughters? Will one of them marry Mr Laurence's grandson?'

Meg heard these words and she was very upset.

'I like Laurie very much,' she thought. 'But I do not want to marry him. We don't think about Laurie's money. He is our best friend.'

Meg went home. She spoke to her mother.

'Marmee, do you have marriage-plans for us?' she asked.

'Marriage-plans?' said Mrs March.

Meg told her mother all about the women's conversation. Mrs March was very angry.

'Those women are very foolish,' she said. 'My daughters are beautiful and good and happy. They will marry good husbands.'

'But good men are not always rich men,' Mrs March said. 'Love is more important than money. Don't marry a rich man without love, Meg. Marry a poor man with love. Then you will be happy.'

'You're right, Marmee,' Meg said. 'I'll always remember your words.'

———

The next day, a letter arrived for Jo. Jo read the letter to her sisters.

Dear Jo,

Tomorrow, some new friends will come to visit me. We will go on a picnic by the river. I have two boats. We will have a good day. John Brooke, my teacher will come with us. Please come. And please bring Meg, Beth and Amy too.

Best wishes, Laurie

'A picnic! That will be exciting!' said Amy. 'Please, Marmee, we want to go on the picnic.'

'Very well. Go on the picnic,' said Mrs March. 'You will have a good time.'

The next day was warm and sunny. Laurie and his new friends walked to the river. The March girls met them there. They all brought baskets of food. They put the baskets into the two small boats. The March sisters sat in the boats. Laurie and his friends rowed the boats on the river. Then they got out and they found a good place for the picnic. Everybody was hungry and the food was delicious.

Later, Jo, Laurie, Beth and Amy talked to Laurie's friends and they played games.

Meg was reading a German book. She did not understand some of the words. Mr Brooke, Laurie's teacher, understood German. He helped Meg with the words.

Mr Brooke was a quiet young man. He had brown eyes and a kind face. He often looked at Meg. But Meg did not see him looking at her.

'You're a very good teacher, Mr Brooke,' said Meg.

'Thank you,' replied Mr Brooke. 'I enjoy my work. Laurie is a very good student.'

Everybody had a good time at the picnic. At last, they had to go home.

The next day, Meg was looking for her gloves.

'I've lost a glove,' she said. 'Have you seen it, Jo?'

'No, I haven't seen it,' replied Jo. 'Did you lose it at the picnic? I'll ask Laurie.'

Later, Jo said to Laurie, 'Meg has lost a glove.'

Laurie started to laugh. 'I know where her glove is,' he said.

'Where is it?' asked Jo.

'I will tell you,' said Laurie. 'But don't tell Meg.'

'I won't tell Meg,' said Jo.

'The glove is in John Brooke's pocket,' said Laurie.

Jo did not understand. 'What do you mean?' she said. 'Why is the glove in John Brooke's pocket?'

'Meg dropped her glove and John Brooke found it,' said Laurie. 'He put the glove in his pocket. He looks at it every day. John is in love with Meg. Isn't that wonderful?'

But Jo was angry and upset. 'No,' she said. 'It isn't wonderful. It's terrible news. Mr Brooke will marry Meg. He will take her away from us. No, I am not happy! I am very unhappy!'

7

A Telegram

Summer and autumn passed. It was November. The weather was cold and wet.

One afternoon, the March sisters were sitting in their living-room. Meg looked out of the window. She watched the rain.

'November is a terrible month,' she said. 'It is cold and wet. Nothing ever happens. Our lives are very boring. And we have no money.'

Amy was painting a picture.

'One day I'll be a famous artist,' she said. 'I'll travel to Italy. I'll paint beautiful pictures. Then I'll sell the pictures. And we will have lots of money.'

'I'm going to write books,' said Jo. 'I'll be rich and famous too. That is my dream. What is your dream Beth?'

'I'm very happy now,' said Beth. 'I shall stay at home with Marmee and Father.'

Meg looked out of the window again. Suddenly, she said, 'There's Laurie. He's coming to the front door.'

A few moments later, Laurie came into the room. He was holding a small envelope in his hand. He was worried and upset.

'What is it, Laurie?' said Jo. 'Is something wrong?'

'Where is Mrs March?' said Laurie. 'I have come from the Post Office.'

Laurie held up the envelope. 'This is a telegram for your mother. It's from Washington,' he said.

At that moment, Mrs March came into the room. Laurie gave her the telegram. Mrs March opened it and she read it quickly. Then she sat down in a chair. Her face was white.

THE AMERICAN TELEGRAPH COMPANY.

Dated ...... *Washington* *14th* 1863
Rec'd. Boston ...... *November* *14th* 1863
To ...... *Mrs M. March* ......

Your husband is very ill.
He is in this hospital.
Come immediately.
P. Dale, The Army Hospital,
Washington

39

'I must go to Washington,' said Mrs March. 'I will go on the train tomorrow morning. Jo, run to the Post Office. Send a telegram to the hospital. Send this reply – "I will come immediately." Meg, Beth, Amy, come and help me. I have to pack my case.'

The three girls started to help their mother. Jo put on her hat and she went out. Laurie went home.

Mrs March went to her desk in the living-room. She opened a drawer. There was some money in the drawer. She looked at the money. There was not very much.

'I have to buy a train ticket,' she thought. 'Will the girls have enough money for food?'

A few minutes, later there was a knock on the front door. Meg opened the door. Old Mr Laurence and Mr Brooke, Laurie's teacher, were standing outside.

'Laurie told us the bad news about your father,' said Mr Laurence. 'I'm very sorry. Will your mother go to Washington?'

'Yes,' said Meg. 'She will go to Washington tomorrow morning.'

'She must not go alone,' said Mr Laurence. 'A friend must go with her. I'm an old man. I am not strong. I can't go with her. But John Brooke is a young man. He can go to Washington with your mother.'

Mr Brooke looked at Meg and he smiled. His face was very kind. 'Don't worry about your mother,' he said. 'I'll take care of her.'

Meg was very pleased.'

Thank you very, very much,' she said.

Soon everything was ready for Mrs March's journey. Evening came. But Jo had not returned. Mrs March was worried.

'Where is Jo?' she said. 'It's very late.'

At last, Jo came home. She walked into the kitchen and she put some money on the table.

'This money is for your journey, Marmee,' she said.

Mrs March looked at the money. Then she looked at Jo. She was very surprised.

'Twenty-five dollars!' she said. 'Jo, where did you get this money?'

Jo did not answer. She took off her hat. Everybody looked at her. Jo's hair was very short.

'Your hair! Your beautiful red hair!' said Meg. 'Oh, Jo, what have you done?'

'Many women want long red hair,' said Jo. 'I went to the barber's shop. The barber cut my hair. Then I sold him my hair. He gave me twenty-five dollars for it. I wanted to help Marmee and Father.'

Tears fell from Mrs March's eyes.

'Jo, you are good and kind,' she said.

———

That night, Meg and Jo could not sleep. Jo was thinking about her hair. Meg was thinking about Mr Brooke. Both girls were worrying about their father.

The next morning, Mr Laurence's carriage came to the Marches' house. Mr Brooke was sitting inside the carriage. Mrs March kissed her daughters and she said goodbye. Then she got into the carriage.

The sun shone on the sad faces of the March sisters.

'Goodbye, dear Marmee,' they said. 'Goodbye!'

8

Beth Is Ill

Mrs March was in Washington. The four sisters worked very hard. They did the housework every day. They were worried about their father and mother. But the girls were very kind to each other. And they wrote to their mother every day.

Soon a letter arrived from Mrs March.

My dear daughters,
I have some wonderful news.
Father is getting better. But he is
not strong. He has to stay in
hospital for some weeks. Then
Mr Brooke and I will bring him
home. Don't worry, little daughters.
Take care of each other. Soon
we will all be together again.
Your loving Marmee

The girls were happy. And soon, Meg, Jo and Amy forgot about the housework. Beth did not forget. She did her own work, and she did her sisters' work too.

One afternoon, Beth, Meg and Jo were talking. Amy was not at home.

'Meg,' said Beth. 'Please will you visit the Hummel family? Marmee often visits them. Marmee is not here. We must visit the Hummels.'

'I'm sorry, Beth. I'm very tired today,' said Meg. 'Jo must go to the Hummels' house.'

'I can't go,' said Jo. 'I'm going to meet Laurie. I can't visit the Hummels today. You must go yourself, Beth.'

'I've visited the Hummels every day this week,' said Beth. 'The baby is ill and I am very worried.'

'Oh,' said Meg. 'Amy will come home soon. Then she must visit the Hummels.'

An hour passed, but Amy did not come home. Meg and Jo went upstairs. Meg looked at a new dress. Jo wrote a story. They forgot about the Hummels. Beth waited. At last, she put on her coat. She put some food in a basket and she went out. Meg and Jo did not see her leaving.

Later, Beth returned. She did not speak to anybody. She went upstairs to her mother's bedroom and she shut the door.

An hour later, Jo found Beth. Beth was sitting on her mother's bed. Her face was white. And she was crying. She was holding a bottle of medicine.

'What is wrong?' Jo asked.

'Oh, Jo, the baby is dead!' said Beth.

'Which baby?' asked Jo.

'The Hummel baby,' replied Beth. 'I went to the Hummels' house this afternoon. The baby was very ill. Mrs Hummel went to get the doctor. I held the baby in my arms, but it died.'

'Oh, Beth, that is terrible!' said Jo. 'What happened next?'

'Mrs Hummel came back with the doctor,' said Beth. 'The doctor looked at the baby. He said, "This baby had scarlet fever."'

'Scarlet fever!' said Jo.

'Yes,' Beth said. 'The doctor gave me this medicine. He said, "Go home immediately. Drink some of this." And now I have a headache and I'm very hot.'

Suddenly, Jo was afraid. 'Has Beth got scarlet fever?' she thought. 'It is a very dangerous illness.'

'Don't worry, Beth,' Jo said. 'I'll tell Meg. We will get Marmee's doctor.'

Meg was very worried. 'Beth went to the Hummels' house every day,' she said to Jo. 'We must get Doctor Bangs immediately.'

Doctor Bangs came and he looked at Beth.

Then the doctor spoke to Meg and Jo.

'Beth has scarlet fever,' he said. 'Who will take care of her?'

'We will,' said Meg. 'Jo and I have had scarlet fever. We are safe.'

'Has Amy had scarlet fever?' asked Dr Bangs.

'Amy hasn't had the fever,' replied Meg. 'She will not be safe here. She must stay with father's aunt, Aunt March.'

'Good,' said Doctor Bangs. 'Take care of Beth. I'll come again tomorrow.'

The doctor left the house. Jo spoke to Meg.

'We must write to Marmee,' she said. 'We must tell her about Beth.'

'No,' said Meg. 'Marmee is taking care of Father. She can't come home now. Marmee must stay in Washington. We must not tell her about Beth.'

Jo started to cry.

'Washington is many miles away,' she said. 'We were wrong, Meg. We didn't visit the Hummels. Beth went there every day. And now she has scarlet fever. Oh, Meg, what are we going to do?'

Meg put her arms round Jo.

'Don't cry, Jo,' she said. 'Beth has scarlet fever. But she will get better soon. Now we must take care of her.'

The next day, Amy went to Aunt March's house. Meg and Jo took care of Beth.

9

News from Washington

Beth was very ill. The days passed and she did not get better.

Beth could not eat. She slept for many hours. Sometimes she was awake, but she could not remember things. Sometimes, she called Jo, 'Meg'. Sometimes, she called Meg, 'Jo'.

Beth said her mother's name, again and again. Jo and Meg were worried and afraid.

One morning, the two girls were talking.

'Let's send a telegram to Marmee,' said Jo. 'Let's tell her about Beth now. Then she will come home.'

'All right,' said Meg. She sat down and she wrote the words for a telegram.

DEAREST MARMEE.

BETH HAS SCARLET FEVER. SHE IS VERY ILL. PLEASE COME HOME IMMEDIATELY.
YOUR LOVING DAUGHTERS
MEG AND JO.

'I'll take this to the Post Office this afternoon,' said Meg.

But that afternoon, a letter arrived from Mrs March. There was bad news in the letter. Mr March was very ill again.

Meg and Jo read the letter. They looked at each other.

'We must not send the telegram to Marmee,' said Meg. 'Beth is ill, but Father is ill too. Marmee must stay with him. She can't come home now.'

_____

A week later, it was the first day of December. The weather was very cold. The wind blew all day and snow fell.

In the morning, Dr Bangs visited the house. He looked at Beth for a long time. Then he spoke to Meg and Jo.

'Beth is very, very ill,' he said. 'Your mother must to come home immediately. I will come back tonight.'

'Meg,' said Jo. 'We must send the telegram to Marmee.'

Jo put on her coat and hat and she ran outside. Laurie was walking towards the house. He was holding a letter in his hand. He was very happy and excited.

'I have good news,' he said. 'This letter is from John Brooke. Your father is getting better now. But what's wrong, Jo? Where are you going?'

'I'm going to send a telegram to Marmee,' replied Jo. 'Doctor Bangs visited Beth. She is very, very ill.' Jo started to cry.

Laurie held Jo's hand. 'Dear Jo,' he said. 'Grand-father and I will always help you. Please remember that.'

'Yes,' said Jo. 'You are our good friends. Thank you very much.'

'I must tell you something,' said Laurie. 'Last week, Grandfather and I were talking about Beth. We were very worried about her. We sent a telegram to your mother. We told her about Beth's illness. Today, I received this letter from John Brooke. Your mother will be here early tomorrow morning. Then everything will be all right.'

Jo was happy again. She stopped crying. 'Laurie,' she said. 'You're a wonderful friend. Thank you.'

Jo ran inside the house. She told Meg the good news. Meg was very happy too.

———

The afternoon passed slowly. Beth lay in her bed. Her eyes were closed. She did not eat or speak. Sometimes she drank some water. Meg and Jo sat by her bed. The wind blew and the snow fell. At last, night came. Meg and Jo watched Beth. They waited for Mrs March. And they waited for Doctor Bangs.

Old Mr Laurence and Laurie waited too. They sat downstairs in the living-room. They sat by the fire.

The hours passed. At two o'clock in the morning, Jo went to the window. She looked out at the garden. There was thick snow everywhere.

'The world is sad and lonely tonight!' she thought. Suddenly, she heard a noise. She turned round. Meg was crying.

'Beth has died,' thought Jo. 'Beth has died and Meg cannot tell me.'

She went to the bed and looked down at Beth. Beth was quiet. Her eyes were closed.

Then the door opened and Dr Bangs came into the room.

'Beth is dead,' Jo said quietly.

Dr Bangs looked at Beth. He held her hands. Then he smiled.

'No,' he said. 'Beth isn't dead. She's sleeping. She's going to be all right. There is no more danger.'

Meg and Jo put their arms round each other and they cried. They were very, very happy.

Soon it was morning. The sisters heard the sound of a carriage in the street.

Then Laurie called from the living-room. 'Girls! Girls! Your mother is here!'

Mrs March had come home.

10

The Best Christmas Present

Amy was unhappy at Aunt March's house. She wanted to see her family. Aunt March was an old lady. She did not like young girls. Sometimes she was angry with Amy.

Every evening, Amy had to read to Aunt March. But she did not like Aunt March's books. They were not very interesting.

One evening, Aunt March spoke to Amy.

'I have had a letter from your mother,' she said. 'She has come home. She will take you home tomorrow.'

Amy was very happy.

Soon the four sisters were together again. And every day, Beth was stronger.

————

One day, a letter came from Washington. It was from John Brooke. Mrs March read the letter.

'Girls, girls, I have wonderful news!' she said. 'Mr Brooke is going to bring Father home.'

————

It was a week before Christmas. The March sisters were very busy and excited. They made Christmas presents. And they cooked delicious food for Christmas Day.

In the evening, Jo spoke to her mother.

'Marmee,' she said. 'I must tell you something. John Brooke loves Meg. In the summer, Meg lost a glove. John Brooke found it and he put it in his pocket. Isn't that terrible, Marmee?'

'Why is it terrible?' asked Mrs March.

'John Brooke will marry Meg,' replied Jo. 'He'll take her away from us.'

'Listen, Jo,' said Mrs March. 'John Brooke is a good young man. He was very kind and helpful in Washington.'

'John Brooke must not marry Meg,' Jo said. 'Meg must not marry a poor man.'

'Money is not important,' replied Mrs March. 'John is good and kind. He loves Meg very much. But Meg is young. She is only seventeen. They must wait.'

'Please don't be sad, Jo,' Mrs March said. 'One day, you will leave this house too. You will meet a good man and you will marry him.'

'No, mother!' cried Jo. 'I'll never marry anybody! I want to be a famous writer.'

———

At last it was Christmas Day. Everybody had some presents. Everybody was happy.

In the afternoon, Laurie and old Mr Laurence came to the Marches' house. They brought presents. Everybody talked and everybody laughed.

Then, somebody knocked at the front door. Laurie went to the door. A moment later, he came back into the living-room. He was very excited.

'Here is another Christmas present for the March family!' he said.

A tall man was standing behind Laurie. Everybody looked at the man. For a moment, they did not speak. Then the girls shouted together, 'Father!'

All the sisters ran to their father. They put their arms round him. Everybody was talking and crying.

'This is the best Christmas present!' said Amy.

Then another man came into the room. It was John Brooke. Meg ran to towards him.

'I'm very happy to see you, John,' she said. 'Thank you! You have brought Father home to us!'

Later, everybody ate Christmas dinner. Then the Laurences and John Brooke went home. The March family sat by the fire.

Mr March looked at the faces of his four happy daughters.

'My dears,' he said. 'This year has been very long and difficult. You had to work very hard. I left home and you were girls. Now you have grown up. You are four fine women.'

11

A Happy Ending

The Marches were together again. Every day, Mr March and Beth were stronger.

Laurie and old Mr Laurence often visited the Marches. But John Brooke did not come with them. Meg was sad. She wanted to see John very much.

'I don't understand,' she thought. 'Why doesn't John visit us?'

One afternoon, Meg and Jo were talking. Jo saw an umbrella by the front door.

'Whose umbrella is that?' she asked. 'I've never seen it before.'

'It's John Brooke's umbrella,' replied Meg. 'He left it here on Christmas Day. He has forgotten it.'

'Meg,' said Jo. 'Do you like John Brooke? Do you love him? Are you going to marry him?'

'No, no!' Meg said. 'I'm too young for marriage. Please don't ask me these questions, Jo.'

'Then you don't love him?' said Jo.

'Oh – I don't know!' said Meg.

Jo looked out of the window.

'Meg, John Brooke is outside now,' she said. 'He is coming to the front door. You don't love him, Meg. He must go away. Please tell him!'

Meg ran to the stairs. She wanted to hide in her

bedroom. But it was too late. John Brooke came into the house!

'Good afternoon,' John said. 'Do you have my umbrella? I left it here.' He smiled. Then he said, 'How is your father?'

'He's very well, thank you,' said Jo. 'We'll bring him.'

Jo went upstairs and Meg started to follow. But John Brooke stopped her.

'Please don't go, Meg,' he said. 'I must say some-thing to you.'

'Oh,' said Meg. 'Let's talk in the living-room.'

John and Meg went into the living-room. Meg sat down and John Brooke sat beside her. He held her hand.

'Dearest Meg,' he said. 'I love you. I am poor, but I can work hard. I can make a good home for you. Please, Meg, will you be my wife?'

At first, Meg did not speak. Then she said, 'I don't know, John.'

'Please, Meg,' said John Brooke. 'Will you marry me?'

Suddenly, the door opened and Aunt March came into the room. Meg and John were very surprised. Aunt March was surprised too!

'Good afternoon, Meg,' she said. 'Where is your father?' Then she looked at John Brooke. 'Who is this young man?'

'Aunt March, this is John Brooke,' Meg said. 'John is Father's friend.'

'John Brooke!' said Aunt March. 'Why are you here, young man? What are you talking about?'

'Aunt March,' said Meg quietly. 'John Brooke wants to marry me.'

Aunt March looked angrily at John Brooke. Then she said, 'Young man, Mrs March has spoken about you. You are poor. You have no money. Meg must marry a man with money.'

Meg was very angry.

'Aunt March,' she said. 'John is poor, but he is a good man and I love him.'

John Brooke smiled and his eyes were bright.

'Thank you, dearest Meg,' he said. 'Do you love me? Will you marry me?'

'Yes, I will,' said Meg.

'Meg!' said Aunt March. 'You are a very foolish girl. You will never get any money from me. Goodbye!' She turned round and went quickly out of the room.

Meg and John told the March family their good news.

'It's wonderful news,' said Mr and Mrs March. 'Congratulations!'

'Congratulations!' said Amy and Beth together.

Jo said nothing. She was not happy.

Later, Laurie and Mr Laurence came to the house. They congratulated Meg and John. But Laurie looked at Jo's face.

'What's wrong, Jo?' asked Laurie. 'Aren't you happy?'

'No,' said Jo. 'Meg is my dear sister and my dear friend. Now John Brooke will take her away.'

'Jo,' said Laurie. 'You love Meg. She is your sister. But John loves her too. Meg will be happy with John. And, Jo, I'll always be your friend.'

'That's true,' said Jo. 'Thank you, Laurie.'

Jo looked round the room. She looked at her family. Mr and Mrs March were talking together. Amy was sitting on the floor near Meg and John. Beth was talking to old Mr Laurence.

Suddenly, Jo was not sad any more. She turned to Laurie.

'You are right, Laurie,' she said. 'One day, Meg will marry John. But she will always be my sister. We will always love each other.'

'That's right, Jo,' said Laurie.

Jo went over to Meg. She held Meg's hands and she kissed her face.

'Congratulations, dearest Meg,' she said. 'I am very happy for you. And congratulations, John. You are our brother now. Welcome to our family.'

Macmillan Heinemann English Language Teaching, Oxford

A division of Macmillan Publishers Limited

Companies and representatives throughout the world

ISBN 0 435 27334 5

Heinemann is a registered trade mark of Reed Educational & Professional Publishing Ltd

This retold version for Heinemann E L T Guided Readers
Text © Anne Collins 1997
Design and illustration © Reed Educational and
Professional Publishing Limited 1997
First published 1997

Acknowledgements: The publishers would like to thank Popperfoto
for permission to reproduce the picture on page 4.

Illustrated by Barry Wilkinson. Map on page 3 by John Gilkes
Typography by Adrian Hodgkins
Designed by Sue Vaudin
Cover by Peter Sutton and Marketplace Design
Typeset in 12/16 Goudy
Printed and bound in Spain by Mateu Cromo

99 00 10 9 8 7 6 5 4 3 2